Improvement in 3-D

Book 2

DUE DILIGENCE

Moving from Obligation to Opportunity Workbook

Due Diligence

Amy K. Atcha

Improvement in 3-D

Book 2

DUE DILIGENCE
Moving from Obligation to Opportunity Workbook

Due Diligence

Due Diligence: Moving from Obligation to Opportunity Workbook
By: Amy K. Atcha

Copyright 2014 Customized Caring, Inc.

Cover design by: Wayne Johnson

Published by: Customized Caring Publishing
ISBN – 13: 978-0692217597

For information about special discounts on bulk purchases,
Contact Customized Caring, Inc. at 630.306.4480 or www.customizedcaring.com.

About this Book

The Due Diligence: Moving from Obligation to Opportunity workbook is part of the Improvement in 3-D series. It has been designed to provide you with the opportunity to absorb the concepts, acquire the skills and advance your techniques, taking an active role in creating your leadership style. With Improvement in 3-D, you will learn, grow, and enhance your own delegation, due diligence and decision making abilities, as well as assisting those around you. As you study and strengthen your own skills, you will become more creative, more productive and more successful!

As a person, a group member, and as a leader, the information and questions in these books are designed to get you thinking. The exercises are designed to help you practice and implement new methods, expanding your gallery of techniques in all kinds of ways - personally, professionally, in your family, your work or any organization. You will be amazed as you watch your own skills grow to new heights, right along with those around you. Your attitude and style as a leader will never be the same.

The Improvement in 3-D workbooks are effective tools for learning, assessing, strategizing, and practicing methods and techniques. You can use these books for individual training and development, or with a group, to increase your productivity.

The information, tools and tips in these books will stay with you (and your organization) long after you finish the series. Use the guidance, structures and approaches over and over.

Are you ready to start? It's time for Improvement in 3-D!

Due Diligence

Moving from Obligation to Opportunity Workbook

Contents

Due Diligence

Preface

Whether it's your first day on the job, your 20th year of helping out an organization, or you just need a bit more personal development in your life, it's never too soon (or too often!) for Improvement.

Improvement comes in many forms – mental, physical, structural and systematic – just to name a few. It can be achieved individually, in a group, and even as an organization. The great learners and scholars, along with entrepreneurs and businesspeople, never stop improving on themselves, their products, their thinking and their companies.

With each step that you take, you will grow, <u>and</u> seek out even more ways to improve. Soon, you will conceptualize, then visualize, strategize and formulate, and finally implement ways for Improvement.

The second of this three part series on Improvement is on Due Diligence. It may be considered a stand-alone segment or a step on your journey to improve. Either way, it will continue your thinking, planning and working in a more productive and successful manner.

As Franklin Johnson said, "Until we do our due diligence, no one knows, … Once you get in there, who knows. If they're enthusiastic, they might want to go for more."

Moving Due Diligence from merely an obligation into an opportunity is best expressed by Josh S. Hinds when he said, "Doing what's expected of you can make you good, but it's the time you spend going above and beyond what's required that makes you great!"

Thinking in 3-D conjures up many images – many dimensions – of the same, yet different, perspectives. When we think 3-D, we create a structure in our minds that references length, width and depth. In terms of working and creating, we may operate in 3-D:

>   1-D: doing it your way

>   2-D: asking others how they do it

>   **3-D: working together to create a GREAT process, a GREAT product, a GREAT team**

The same goes for our Delegation, our Due Diligence and our Decision Making.

>   Delegation – up, down and across

>   Due Diligence from a variety of sources

>   Decision Making, not just at one level, but considering other factors includes resources (time, money, people), style and method.

Throughout your work in this Improvement in 3-D Series, practice thinking in all three capacities, work on different levels and with different perspectives, and build on your success through knowledge, training and result!

The sections of this book will provide you with basic information and guidance about the concept and reasoning behind due diligence, as well as the steps and instructions for some of the best approaches to performing due diligence. At the back are Tools you can use to begin (or enhance) your due diligence skills.

What is DUE DILIGENCE? gives you the context in which we will use Due Diligence for this book.

Breaking It Down describes the five W's and one big How behind the technique of Due Diligence. Here we will also discuss presenting our evidence and making the "Shift". This section takes you step by step through the various aspects of the process, along with providing you useful techniques and exercises to move you towards opportunity.

Mastering the Move lets you practice the skills by trying out the techniques with simulations and scenarios.

Helpful Tools are resources provided for future study, practice and use.

It's time to Open Up to Opportunity is your call to action!

Now is the time to absorb the knowledge.

Now is the time to enhance your abilities.

Now is the time to leverage your leadership potential.

Now is the time for Improvement in 3-D!

Due Diligence

What is DUE DILIGENCE?

Due Diligence, according to Black's Law Dictionary, is "the diligence reasonably expected from, and ordinarily exercised by, a person who seeks to satisfy a legal requirement or to discharge an obligation." The dictionary further states that "ordinary diligence is the diligence that a person of average prudence would exercise in handling his or her own property like that at issue."

So what does this mean? What exactly is due diligence? How is it done? And why?

In a word, due diligence is Investigating. It's finding out the who, what, where and when (and even why!) of things – transactions, assets or people. It's finding out what makes things work, what the underlying components are, and how the pieces fit together to form a seemingly flawless event.

In most instances, we think of Due Diligence in the context of business or business transactions. We also tend to think of Due Diligence as being the "requirement" to properly justify why we did (or did not) take a specific action. It is the basis, or the underlying information and support that we use to make our decisions.

But could it be more? Could it be the beginning point to improvement in process? In structure? In finances? Yes, yes, it can!

The key to understanding Due Diligence, and the ability to benefit from it – to move from merely an obligation to a true opportunity - lies in the perspective.

A minimum amount of due diligence is prudent (meaning circumspect or judicious in one's dealings; cautious). It is getting the basic facts, the bare minimum of details surrounding the issue at hand.

To do the bare minimum, means to just do enough to get by. It is the least amount of evidence and information needed to have a transaction (or a process) pass inspection. Thinking in "school terms", it is simply the least amount needed to get a "D" grade - after all that is still passing (although hopefully not what you are striving for!).

However, if we take our Due Diligence one step farther, reaching a little deeper, thinking a bit broader, analyzing more of the details, the people, the process, the asset – we might find that Opportunity is lying right at our feet.   It is ripe for the taking!

Therefore, to move from a perspective of obligation to opportunity might be as simple as a mind shift, and analyzing data from a different angle.   It may mean gathering more information, or simply reviewing the information in a different way – with a different purpose in mind, and with a different plan for reaching success.

The basic purpose behind Due Diligence is in fact to support our decisions, our transactions, our processes. However, while Due Diligence can simply stand alone as an Obligation or task to be done, it can benefit us more to think of it in terms of your leadership potential.

Due Diligence as a leadership principle is important for 1) accuracy, 2) completeness, 3) competitiveness, and for 4) resource utilization. The benefits of Due Diligence are vast for the leader, for the staff performing the duty and for the organization in whole.

In addition, other areas are affected when conducing due diligence. To be thorough, the process involves research, training, and goal setting. Finally, for our discussion to be fluid and move along the continuum, we must also deliberate on the difference between an Obligation and an Opportunity.

With Due Diligence not only can you gain an understanding of the unique, concrete transaction at issue, but also of the industry, the environment and the relationship that one transaction has to you and your company. Through leadership and due diligence, you can provide (and receive) professional development and personal growth, as well as a better appreciation and use of time and other resources. Due Diligence can help you, your team and your organization run more efficiently and productively.

To gain the most out of a due diligence experience, YOU must know what you aim to obtain or achieve out of the arrangement. By having a personal and/or professional goal attached to each due diligence assignment, you will have "skin in the game", be committed to the project, AND personally benefit.

Due Diligence is a tool that leaders (and managers) use for a variety of reasons. The key to successful due diligence, however, is that it is done purposefully, with a goal in mind. Simply doing the minimum, only what is necessary to meet a deadline or criteria is not the BEST due diligence, and is not going to move you towards Opportunity. With a change in perspective, and a few extra steps, you can move from obligation to opportunity, thus saving you money, time and resources, and leading to even greater opportunity and growth. Taking those extra steps, going that extra mile, will help you succeed!

Since Due Diligence and its association with Leadership can mean different things to different people, let's start with a brief discussion and exercise.

Due Diligence

Due Diligence is basically like investigating. It is the support and basis for the decisions that we make.

When I think of Due Diligence, I think of:

1.

2.

3.

Leadership

Leadership has many characteristics. We tend to think of Leaders as managers, bosses or superiors. We think of Leaders as the person who is responsible for "getting the job done".

What is leadership?

1.

2.

3.

Due Diligence & Leadership – the Obligation perspective

Leadership and Due Diligence are intertwined.

As an Obligation, why is Due Diligence beneficial to Leaders?

1.

2.

3.

Due Diligence & Leadership – the Opportunity perspective

Leadership and Due Diligence are intertwined.

As an Opportunity, why is Due Diligence beneficial to Leaders?

1.

2.

3.

Research

Almost every aspect of Due Diligence involves doing research. This gathering of information can be viewed in several ways from very specific details to broader knowledge.

When I think of Research, I think of:

1.

2.

3.

Areas of Research provided through Due Diligence:

1.

2.

3.

<ins>Training</ins>

Training is involved in everything we do that is new to us. Conducting due diligence will require that we learn new skills. Training is involved whether we are new to the experience, just want professional development or working on succession planning. Training never ends!

When I think of Training, I think of:

1.

2.

3.

Areas of Training provided through Due Diligence:

1.

2.

3.

Goal Oriented

Goals are the outcomes we want or expect from a given assignment, task or project. Goals can be personal or professional, tangible or intangible, specific or general. Thinking broadly, goals can include something as simple as "gaining greater, more varied knowledge of the industry".

When I think of a project being goal oriented, I think of:

1.

2.

3.

Goals to be gained from Due Diligence include:

1.

2.

3.

Obligation

Obligation is what is required. It may involve time, money, or simply paper. Obligation is a duty, with no inherent benefit. Nonetheless, if obligated then you must comply.

When I think of Obligation, I think of:

1.

2.

3.

Obligation related to Due Diligence includes:

1.

2.

3.

Opportunity

Opportunity opens doors. Opportunity increases knowledge, exposure and experience. Opportunity can save time and money. Opportunity is what we are all seeking.

When I think of Opportunity, I think of:

1.

2.

3.

Opportunities to be gained from Due Diligence include:

1.

2.

3.

Let's practice. Consider one transaction: Your company, Atlas Electronics, wants to purchase (or lease) new vehicles for its sales team. You have been assigned to conduct the Due Diligence. Fill in the blanks, then let's discuss.

ATLAS ELECTRONICS – NEW CAR DILIGENCE

Simply put, what is needed?

What is our leadership reason for conducting the Due Diligence?

Will we need to do any research before or during our assignment? If so, what?

Is any training needed?

What is our goal related to this Due Diligence?

Describe what Due Diligence is Obligation.

Describe what additional Due Diligence could lead to Opportunity. How?

You've just seen a brief glimpse at the land of Due Diligence – a basic transaction with, purportedly, a basic goal.

But don't stop too early!

Opportunity lies in going the extra mile, thinking in a broader sense and with greater plans. Beyond every requirement lies endless potential for additional savings, information and growth. Sometimes to reach success you need to look past the horizon, into the unknown. Be creative! Be resourceful! Don't quit until you've exhausted your possibilities.

It's not too late to **Move from Obligation to Opportunity!**

Due Diligence

Breaking It Down

In this section, we will work on breaking down the Due Diligence model. We will discuss the **Five W's** and the Big **HOW**? We'll touch on **Presenting** our findings, and especially how to make the **Shift from Obligation to Opportunity**. We will end the chapter with a short discussion of the **Keys to Success**.

The Five W's

We know that due diligence is required, and we even have a general idea of what should be done. As your head starts spinning with the variety of tasks that need to be completed, let's take a look at the Five W's to any good investigation – Who, What, Where, When, and Why.

1. Who?

If you are new to the Due Diligence world, you might wonder Who? is supposed to be gathering all this information we are talking about. You certainly don't consider yourself an expert in every arena. So Who? will be collecting the evidence, the research, and the support you need? Who does Due Diligence?

Remember, good leaders don't do everything themselves. They use others to help – either through delegation or by hiring outsiders. While you are almost always welcome to "gather intel", your function might also simply be as the repository for all the information that is gathered.

List individuals that perform Due Diligence.

1.

2.

3.

4.

5.

6.

2. What?

Next we need to determine **What?** types of information can be obtained. As you may suspect, for each due diligence assignment, the evidence will vary. Be sure to think in different dimensions – structural, transaction, financial, systematic, legal, functional, etc. Let's brainstorm!

List possible types of information we might want to gather.

1.

2.

3.

4.

5.

6.

7.

8.

9

10.

3. Where?

Next, **Where?** can we obtain all this valuable insight? **Where?** can and should we conduct our Due Diligence? In today's world, keep in mind information is virtually everywhere! Think written, electronic, verbal, as well as public, private, governmental….the list goes on.

List possible places to obtain information.

1.

2.

3.

4.

5.

6.

7.

8.

9

10.

4. When?

When? to gather the information is out next decision. There are 4 specific times when Due Diligence is especially important. However, we are not restricted to only these instances.

The 4 specific times when Due Diligence is important are:

1.

2.

3.

4.

Use the following basic chart to track your on-going due diligence efforts. Remember, you may should review your due diligence every 3-5 years for continued justification.

Project	Purpose	Review date	Review date	Review date

5. Why?

We have already touched on our last W – **Why?** in the previous section. So, let's review. For now, keep your thinking in the perspective of Obligation.

Reasons why we conduct Due Diligence:

1.

2.

3.

4.

The HOW

On to the Big question – **HOW** do we do it? How should we (or anyone else for that matter) begin? What specifically should we do?   Where do we begin and How do we know when we are done?

It's always best to start with a plan. Think of what your goal is – what are you trying to support?   You may want to use a simple statement such as:

My due diligence will support the decision to: _____.

Now that you have definitely stated what the purpose is, you can use the GAAGAC approach for performing the work.

Use the GAAGAC approach:

1.   G

2.   A

3.   A

4.   G

5.   A

6.   C

Don't forget to identify and prioritize activities within each part of the plan. It's easy to expend a lot of unnecessary energy and resources stumbling around trying to figure out what to do. Use the Due Diligence Work Plans in the Tools section as a guide.

The Basic Due Diligence Work Plan looks like this:

Project: _____

Anticipated Due Date: _____

My due diligence will support the decision to: _____.

Research needed?   If yes, what?

GAAGAC:
Information to Gather:
       Documents   Interview / Speak with people
       Financial   Transactional Situational
       Legal   Other

Analyze:
       Financial   Transactional Situational
       Legal   Other

Apply against context:
       Financial   Transactional Situational
       Legal   Other

Conclusion:
       Written report with Executive Summary
       Oral presentation with materials

For a more detailed work plan, you will want to make specific lists, so that you are sure to cover all your bases - what documents to get, what analysis to do, and who to talk to (interview). A Detailed Due Diligence Work Plan can be used to accomplish this.

Use your calendar to schedule out research days, interview days, analysis days. Be sure to build in a "buffer" to re-group, re-think, and re-vise your plans and your investigation. You may also find the Priority Chart and Assignment Chart included in the Helpful Tools section to be of value, especially if you have a team working on the project.

Keep in mind that proper Due Diligence takes time. When considering the amount of work to be done, the people involved in conducting the research and the goals to be achieved, you will soon realize that deadlines are appropriate as well as scheduled status meetings. Use the Status Report form in the Helpful Tools section for this portion of the Due Diligence project.

And just when you think you're done, ask yourself one more time – What more do I need?

Presenting the results

We're not done yet. We need to **Present** our findings, and make our recommendation. Use an outline format to articulate the goal, the information gathered, the context and the conclusion.

You may need to provide both a written report and an oral presentation. Your objectives for each of these are different. Your report and presentation should be tailored to the audience to which it will be provided.

For the written report, you will need an executive summary, followed by the detailed information. The executive summary should be only 1-2 pages. The supporting material should be organized and labeled appropriately.

The oral presentation should follow an outline, provide bullet points. Supporting documentation should be presented in summary chart format. Your presentation may also include flowcharts, spreadsheets and charts, provided each is easily explainable, neat and not overly detailed.

Be sure your presentation (and supporting due diligence) pass the "smell" test!

Format for Presenting Findings

Project name: _____

Conclusion: (written in a direct and detailed statement format – one sentence)

Overview of Findings: (Why and how decision was made - paragraph)

Basis of review:
        Purpose?
        Context?
        What was reviewed?
        Who did the review?
        Time period involved?

Benefits identified:

Costs identified:

List of supporting information.
        (Summarize any statistics and/or provide supporting attachments such as charts, spreadsheets, etc.)

How you present is just as important as what you present. Follow the format in your discussions, and anticipate any questions that might be asked.

Let's Shift – Moving from Obligation to Opportunity

Now we move to the focus of this book. It's time to **SHIFT our perspective**. Sure, we've learned that Due Diligence is an obligation to be fulfilled. But let's take it one step farther – let's **Move from Obligation to Opportunity**!

Before we get too far ahead of ourselves, stop and think …   Moving from obligation to opportunity involves a mind shift. You are now looking for ways to improve service, use of resources, superior methods and systems, etc.

What Opportunities are possible?

With a different viewpoint or additional insight (and information) what other improvements exist?

Remember to think in all dimensions - financial, transactional, situational, legal, etc. Consider time, money, use of personnel, out-sourcing, materials, customer service, succession planning, and technology just to name a few.

Conducting limited due diligence on an annual basis can be as simple as reviewing customer service satisfaction results, time management and resource utilization. Opportunities can include DECREASING reporting, services and personnel, as well as INCREASING uses of new technology and enhanced service to customers.

Possible opportunities (benefits) from additional / continued Due Diligence:

1.

2.

3.

4.

5.

6.

7.

8.

9.

10.

Everything comes at a cost. When considering additional due diligence, think about the extra time, money, personnel and other resources you may need to use.

The costs of augmenting the Due Diligence are:

1.

2.

3.

Do the benefits outweigh the cost? It is not always possible to "seize every opportunity" when it is first identified. However, it never hurts to keep a listing of possible additional evaluations that can be done to reap the benefits. You may want to put this list of possibilities into its own "pending activities" chart to review later in the year or as part of a structured review process.

Opportunity	Reason	Time involved	Planned time frame

When assessing the benefits and costs of Opportunity due diligence, it is helpful to keep a running chart of due diligence efforts. It's not so easy to remember when each review was conducted, why, and the resulting action(s). Following are a couple different charts you may want to use.

Transaction	Date reviewed	Reason for review	Result

Project	Purpose	Review date	Review date	Review date

Keys to Success

Purpose

To achieve the greatest rewards and have the most positive experiences (i.e. SUCCESS), it is essential to have AND know the purpose behind what and why you are performing due diligence – especially if you are seeking Opportunities. As you work through your project due diligence plan (yes, you should PLAN prior to gathering information), make a note as to the purpose for each part of the process.

Communication

As with all matters big and small, communication is key. The method as well as the manner in which information is obtained and disseminated can determine the success of the project. Initially you are gathering facts, not creating bias with your own opinions. Conclusions and recommendations are based on sound and proper diligence. Keep respect and OBJECTIVITY at the forefront of any exchanges – written or verbal, individual or group based.

One More Step?

Where to end your Due Diligence efforts is anybody's guess. The proper amount of time to spend, the exact number of analyses to do, and the people to involve will all be relative to the matters at hand. Setting goals and deadlines upfront will help limit the scope of the project. Using a cost/benefit analysis prior to additional work can be a significant savings. There is no limit to the amount of work that can be done, but justifying your time and your expenses helps to keep matters in check.

Patience

We all need to have patience, whether it's at home or at work. Remember, Due Diligence can be subjective. And moving along the spectrum of thinking from obligation to opporuntiy does not happen overnight. You will not know exactly where to stop on your first time, your second time, or maybe ever. The key to remember is to learn along the way, and work to improve and enhance your skills through your experiences. For this, you need Patience.

Due Diligence

Mastering the Move

We've talked about Due Diligence – what it is, what it involves and why it's important, and even broken it down step by step – changing our perspective from Obligation to Opportunity. Now, let's practice.

Following are 3 scenarios. After reading the summary of each, fill in the worksheet that follows.

Scenario One: Cellphone Contracts

The contract for the Phillips Company Copy Service staff cell phone package is due to expire at the end of next year. Recently, you, the Treasurer of Phillips Company, switched to the latest technology for your own cell phone and you're wondering if it makes sense to have all the company phones updated too.

Currently, the company has 57 phones in its contract. The bundle package provides unlimited data and voice on a group rate for all phones at a flat rate of $100 per month per phone. International calling is separate, although last year only 10 people in the company had a need for this service. The original contract was entered into 3 years ago.

Your task is to determine if the phone contract should be renewed at the current rate ($100 per month per phone) or whether a different package, with additional features, and possibly updated hardware, would be better.

Scenario Two: Warehousing Space

Joannie's Trinkets is a small retail store which carries a variety of knick knacks from around the world. Joannie and her 3 employees run the shop.

During the holiday season (November and December) Joannie hires extra help due to increased sales volume. In addition, over the past 5 years, sales have increased almost 5% per year.

The store inventory typically increases beginning in September to prepare for the busy holiday shopping. However, from January through August sales are level, and inventory remains stable.

Joannie's concern is that her current store does not have enough warehousing space to accommodate the increased inventory needs, especially during the last quarter of the year. She is not sure if she needs entirely new space (including a store front) or if she should simply rent additional space for peak inventory times. Currently she is using the extra bedroom in her condominium to store product.

What should Joannie do? What should Joannie consider?

Scenario Three: Outsourced Customer Service Center

Orlando's Servicing (OS) provides an outsourced customer service center for your company, Parity Products (Parity). Parity has been pleased with the service provided by OS thus far. As such, Parity wants to renew its contract for another 2 year commitment, but has asked you to conduct some due diligence to determine if the same contract should be extended or if changes to the terms need to be incorporated.

Parity has provided you with some limited information to get you started with the review.
1. Parity's executives do not need several of the monthly reports that OS currently provides. Other reports and analysis are conducted for Parity by OS, but are billed separately.
2. Parity originally had a 24 hour help line arrangement. However, OS has advised that it typically receives between 3 and 5 calls between the hours of 8 pm and 7 am.
3. OS reports should that wait times for incoming calls received between 9 am and 4 pm exceed 15 minutes. Many customers have complained about the lengthy wait for service.
4. OS pricing is projected to increase by 10% in the upcoming year.

SCENARIO ONE: Cellphone Contracts

What is the goal of the due diligence?

What due diligence is required (obligation)?

What documents/information should be gathered?

What analysis should be conducted?

Is any other research needed? Explain.

What recommendation do you have?

What other opportunities exist at this point?

What will be the advantages? What are the benefits to this opportunity?

What will it cost?

       What additional documents are needed?

       What additional analyses need to be done?

       What additional resources are needed?

       What additional time is required?

Do the benefits outweigh the costs?

Should I review again?   Yes   No
       When? _____

SCENARIO TWO: Warehousing Space

What is the goal of the due diligence?

What due diligence is required (obligation)?

What documents/information should be gathered?

What analysis should be conducted?

Is any other research needed? Explain.

What recommendation do you have?

What other opportunities exist at this point?

What will be the advantages? What are the benefits to this opportunity?

What will it cost?

       What additional documents are needed?

       What additional analyses need to be done?

       What additional resources are needed?

       What additional time is required?

Do the benefits outweigh the costs?

Should I review again?   Yes   No
       When? _____

SCENARIO THREE: Outsourced Customer Service Center

What is the goal of the due diligence?

What due diligence is required (obligation)?

What documents/information should be gathered?

What analysis should be conducted?

Is any other research needed? Explain.

What recommendation do you have?

What other opportunities exist at this point?

What will be the advantages? What are the benefits to this opportunity?

What will it cost?

       What additional documents are needed?

       What additional analyses need to be done?

       What additional resources are needed?

       What additional time is required?

Do the benefits outweigh the costs?

Should I review again?   Yes   No
      When? _____

Due Diligence

Helpful Tools

Due Diligence is not a concrete, rigid process or structure. After all, the Due Diligence that is required, and which you may want to conduct to enhance yourself and your company, will depend on your circumstances, your time frames, your resources, and of course your goals.   No two projects will ever be alike!

However, rather than having to "start at square one" each time, the following Helpful Tools have been developed to offer you a framework for creating your next "Design".

Basic Thought Outline for Due Diligence

Simply put, what is needed?

What is our leadership reason for conducting the Due Diligence?

Will we need to do any research before or during our assignment? If so, what?

Is any training needed?

What is our goal related to this Due Diligence?

Describe what Due **Diligence** is Obligation.

Describe what additional Due Diligence could lead to Opportunity. How?

Basic Due Diligence Work Plan

Project: _____

Anticipated Due Date: _____

My due diligence will support the decision to: _____.

Research needed?   If yes, what?

GAAGAC:
Information to Gather:

          Documents   Interview / Speak with people

Financial   Transactional Situational   Legal   Other

Analyze:
Financial   Transactional Situational   Legal   Other

Apply against context:
Financial   Transactional Situational   Legal   Other

Conclusion:
       Written report with Executive Summary
       Oral presentation with materials

Detailed Due Diligence Work Plan

Project: _____

Anticipated Due Date: _____

Team Leader: _____
Team Members:

This due diligence will support the decision to: _____.

Research needed?   If yes, what?

GAAGAC:
Information to Gather:
        Documents   Interview / Speak with people

Specific documents to obtain:
        Financial –
        Transactional –
        Situational -
        Legal –
        Other –

Electronic documents?   Yes   No

Sources to use:
        Public –
        Private –
        Governmental –

Specific people to contact (name and/or title):

Documents maintained by: _____

Analyses:
    Financial   Transactional Situational   Legal   Other

Spreadsheets should include:

Charts should include:

Comparisons / cross referencing of what:

Other:

Apply against context:
    Financial   Transactional Situational   Legal   Other

Conclusion / Recommendation:
    Written report with Executive Summary
    Oral presentation with materials

Report due date: _____

Presentation date: _____

Status meetings scheduled for the following dates:

Interim due dates for tasks:

**Attach assignment chart, if appropriate

Priority Chart

Assignments to be completed:

Project / Assignment	Time required	Due Date	Priority order

** This priority chart can be used for one person or for one multi-component project.

Assignment Chart

As much as we all want to remember who we delegated what to, when, and deadlines, it may not be possible.

Task	Assigned to	Start date	End date	Status Mtg frequency

** This chart can be sorted by Project, by Person, or by Date.

Status Report – Due Diligence Analysis

Meeting Date: _____   Project: _____

Assigned to: _____   Present at meeting: _____

Goal of project: _____

 Start Date: _____   Projected End Date:_____

Project status as of last meeting (refresh memory)

What information has been gathered since last meeting?

What analysis has been conducted since the last meeting?

What is planned for the upcoming period (week/month/quarter)?

What is still being considered?

Are additional info/ tools/resources needed? What? How much? When?

Is project on target for completion?

Date:	On-target	Ahead	Behind
Cost:	On-target	Ahead	Behind

Continue with due diligence efforts?   Yes   No

Opportunity Evaluation Form – Due Diligence

Date: _____   Project: _____

Start Date: _____   End Date:_____

Required due diligence:

1.

2.

3.

Extra activity and justification (reason and opportunity it will provide):

1.

2.

3.

Overall opinion and comments regarding moving from obligation to opportunity:

_____
_____
_____
_____
_____
_____

Format for Presenting Findings

Project name: _____

Conclusion: (written in a direct and detailed statement format – one sentence)

Overview of Findings: (Why and how decision was made - paragraph)

Basis of review:
      Purpose?
      Context?
      What was reviewed?
      Who did the review?
      Time period involved?

Benefits identified:

Costs identified:

List of supporting information
      (Summarize any statistics and/or provide supporting attachments such as charts, spreadsheets, etc.)

Due Diligence

It's time to Open Up to Opportunity

Now it's time. You've learned what Due Diligence is, how to do it, and what it takes to move from Obligation to Opportunity. You've learned the advantages and costs to a change in perspective. You've been given tools to assist you with your endeavors. Best of all, you've had a chance to get your feet wet by thinking how your shift in perspective can lead to great opportunity, including reduction in time and cost. These concepts can be applied both personally and professionally. Through the exercises in this book, you've even had a chance to put the skills to work by practicing the techniques. You're ready to Move!

Now it's time. Take what you have learned and put it to use. Start RIGHT NOW by jotting down at least 3 due diligence areas that are required, both personally and professionally, that you will work on moving towards opportunity. Stretch your imagination if you have to – believe me, the possibilities are endless. When you are done, you can tear out your list and tack it to your wall.

Now it's time to Open up to Opportunity!

Due Diligence I will do now, searching for Opportunity:

1.

2.

3.

Due Diligence I will schedule out 2 years:

This year (item and month) – obligation and opportunity:

1.

2.

3.

 Next year – obligation and opportunity:

1.

2.

3.

Tips for Successful Due Diligence

1. Be open minded
2. Brainstorm
3. Solicit the help of others
4. Gather first, analyze second
5. Go GAGA (gather, analyze, gather more, analyze more)
6. Consider: price, time, value, volume, flow
7. Don't 'overwork' it – 3-5 may be enough
8. Start with a plan
9. Identify your purpose
10. Summarize your final results
11. Always look for improvements
12. Think beyond what is simply required
13. Flowchart each step in the process or transaction
14. Evaluate annually
15. Evaluate at every significant change
16. Document, document, document
17. Date everything
18. Retain documents for duration of arrangement Plus 10 years
19. Think multi-dimensional
20. Consider the continuum – obligation -----> opportunity

For More Information

Customized Caring, Inc.

901 Indigo Court
Hanover Park, Illinois 60133
www.CustomizedCaring.com

Contact Amy K. Atcha
at
630.306.4480
amy@customizedcaring.com

Life is precious. Take care of those you love.

www.ingramcontent.com/pod-product-compliance
Lightning Source LLC
LaVergne TN
LVHW081321060426
835509LV00015B/1622